Machines
As Tall As
Giants

Machines As Tall As Giants

Paul Stickland

PUFFIN BOOKS

PUFFIN BOOKS
Published by the Penguin Group
Penguin Books USA Inc., 375 Hudson Street, New York, New York 10014
Penguin Books Ltd, Registered Offices: Harmondsworth, Middlesex, England
First published in the United Kingdom by Firefly Books Limited, 1989
Published by Puffin Books, a division of Penguin Books USA Inc., 1996

1   3   5   7   9   10   8   6   4   2

Copyright © Paul Stickland, 1989
Produced by Mathew Price Ltd.
The Old Glove Factory
Bristol Road
Sherborne
Dorset DT9 4 HP
England
ISBN 0-14-055911-6
Printed in China

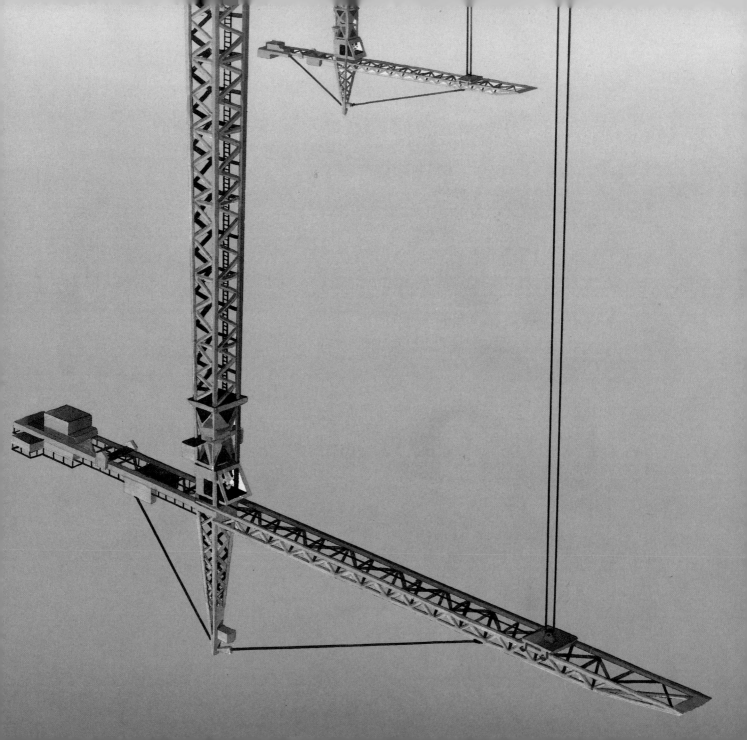

Tower cranes help build skyscrapers by lifting and lowering heavy materials. The cranes are so tall that they have to be built right at the work site. The crane's tower is made taller as the building gets higher.

This mobile crane is lifting a giant piece of concrete that will become part of a bridge. More than ten times the height of a giraffe, the mobile crane can lift objects over two hundred feet off the ground! When its job is finished, the crane just slides back inside itself.

Booster rockets are mounted to the side of this space shuttle. With their amazing power, they help propel the shuttle into outer space. Two minutes after the shuttle is launched, the booster rockets, which are no longer needed, drop off the shuttle.

This giant blast furnace melts down iron to make steel.
Steel is used for building bridges, ships, and cars.
The blast furnace produces heat up to 3,000 degrees
Fahrenheit!

This huge machine loads grain onto ships. First, the machine sends the grain up a conveyor belt. Then the grain winds through a spiral passage in the body of the machine. Finally, the grain drops through long pipes onto the deck of a cargo ship.

A dry dock is a place where ships are built. Inside the dock, shipbuilders put together the hulls of ships before they go to sea. When the ship is assembled, the dock is filled with water to test whether the ship is watertight.

This oil rig drills a hole through the ocean floor to tap an oil deposit deep underground. The oil flows up to the top of the platform like liquid through a drinking straw. This oil rig stands on legs that are over six hundred feet tall, and is as tall as a huge apartment building.

The dockside crane moves up and down
a dock loading and unloading cargo
from ships in the harbor. When it
gets dark, the crane's operator
turns on its big lights, which
are so powerful that they
make night seem like
day again!

These giant silos store cement and sand used to make concrete. The dry materials drop through a large chute into a truck. When the truck is full, water is mixed with the dry matter to make concrete. The truck's enormous drum revolves constantly to keep the concrete from hardening.

This huge car crusher squashes old cars at a junkyard. First, it picks the cars up with its giant claws, then drops them into the machine's mouth. Out come metal cubes!

An astronomer studies the sky through this giant telescope. The telescope magnifies objects, giving the astronomer a close-up view of distant stars and planets. The astronomer hopes to discover new galaxies through the telescope.

This amazing fire engine rescues people trapped in tall buildings during a fire. The fire engine extends its long arm, carrying firefighters up to the windows so they can reach the people trapped inside.

Glossary

astronomer   a scientist who studies stars and planets

blast furnace   a giant oven used to make steel

booster rockets   rockets used to launch a spacecraft

cargo ship   a ship built to carry freight rather than people

conveyor belt   a continuous moving belt driven by rollers that moves objects from one place to another

crane   a machine for lifting and moving objects high off the ground

dry dock   a dock where ships are built and repaired

galaxy   a group of stars in the universe

hull   the main frame of a boat

to launch   to send something into space

silo   a tall container used for storage

space shuttle   a reusable spacecraft that carries people and cargo to and from outer space

telescope   an instrument used by scientists to study stars and planets

watertight   fit together so closely that no water can seep through